General Informa

Terms of Use

This workbook is intended for classroom, homeschool, or personal use only. Reselling, sharing, or modifying it is not permitted by the author. It is copyrighted by Disha Bonner, Oak and Earth Goods.

This material is designed for the age group 4-8 years old.

Connect with us on Social Media

We would love to see your little one enjoying this workbook Tag us on Instagram @oakandearthgoods

Leave us a review!

For any questions or queries contact us, oakandearthgoods@gmail.com

THIS WORKBOOK BELONGS TO:

Table of Content

Table of Content

Table of Content

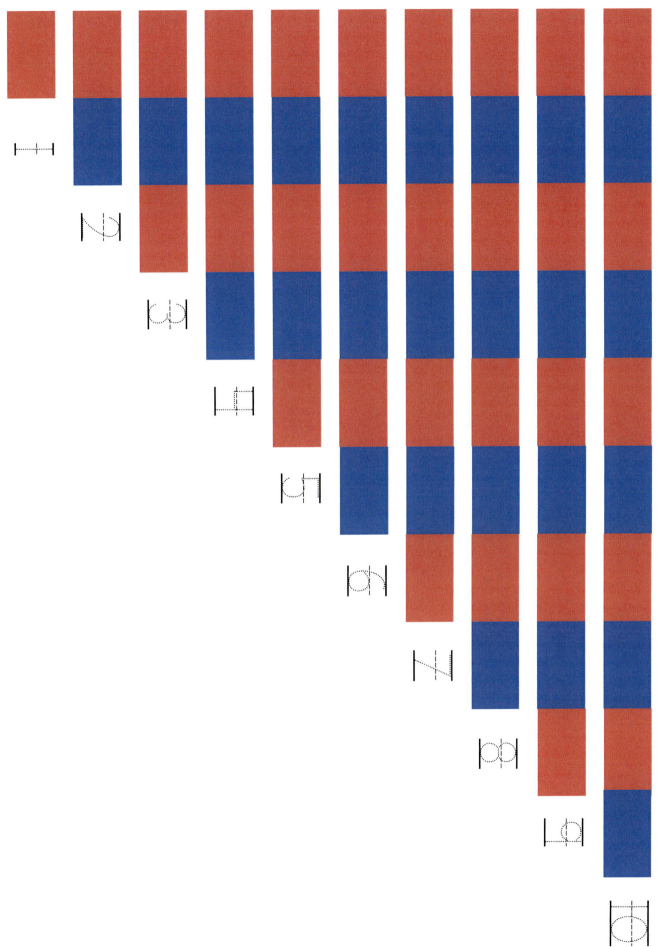

Color the Short Bead Stairs
Montessori Beads

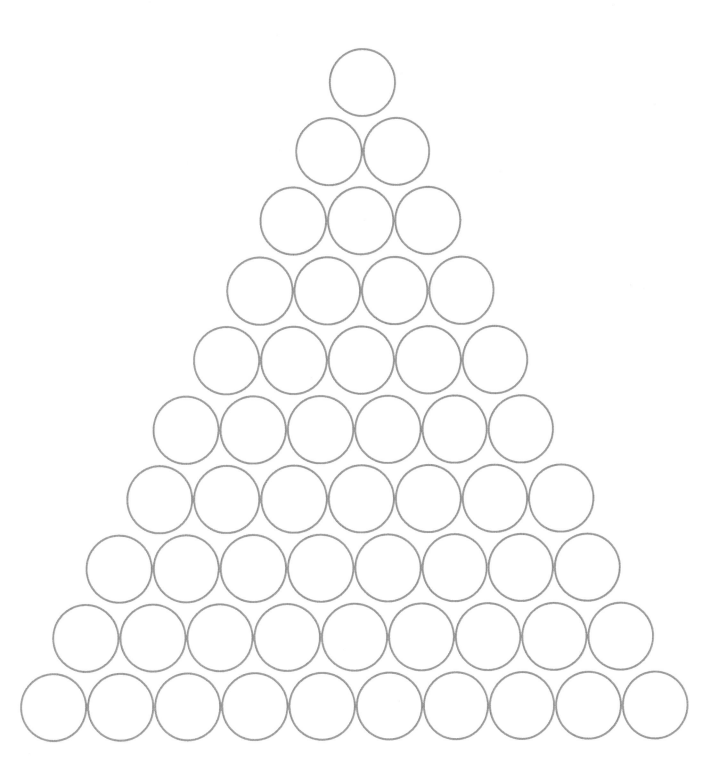

I

one

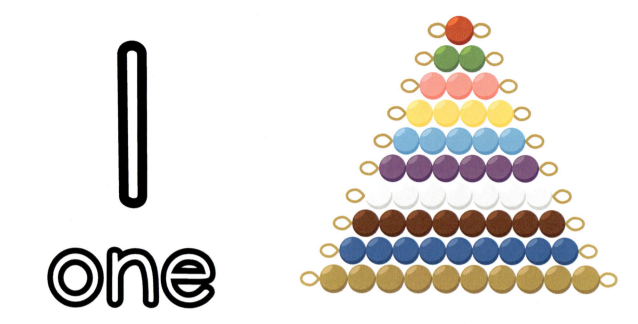

one   one   one

one   one   one

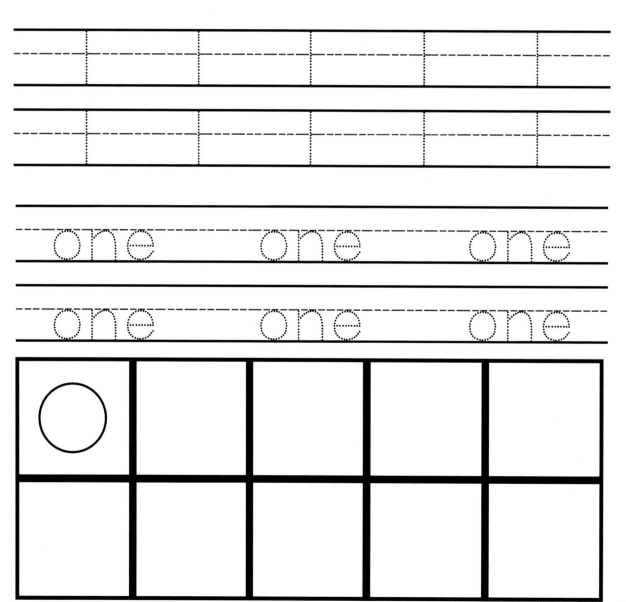

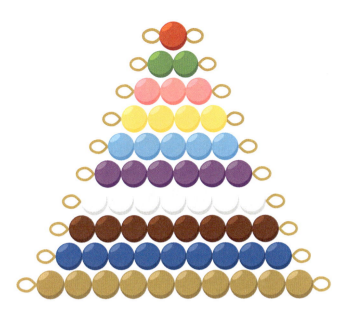

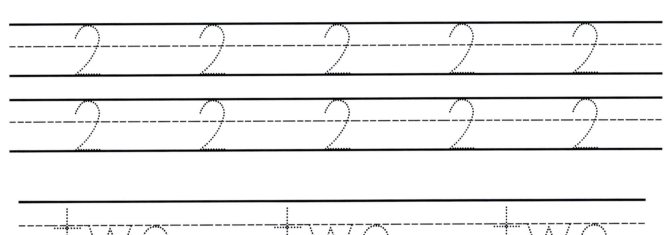

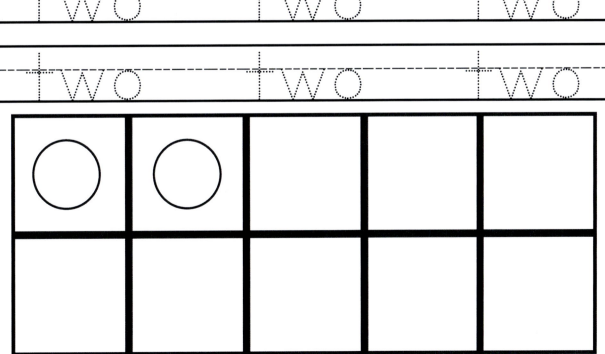

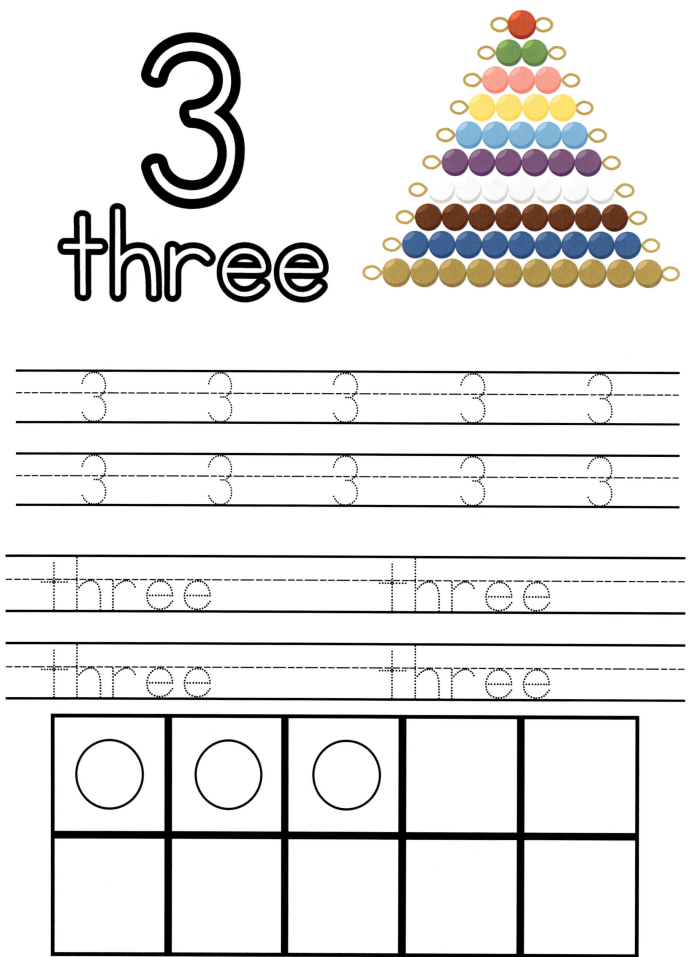

3
three

3 3 3 3 3

3 3 3 3 3

three three

three three

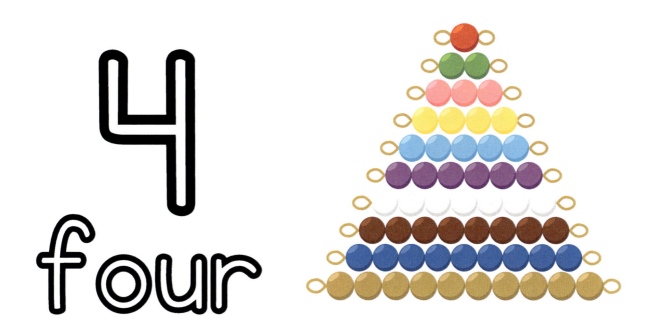

four

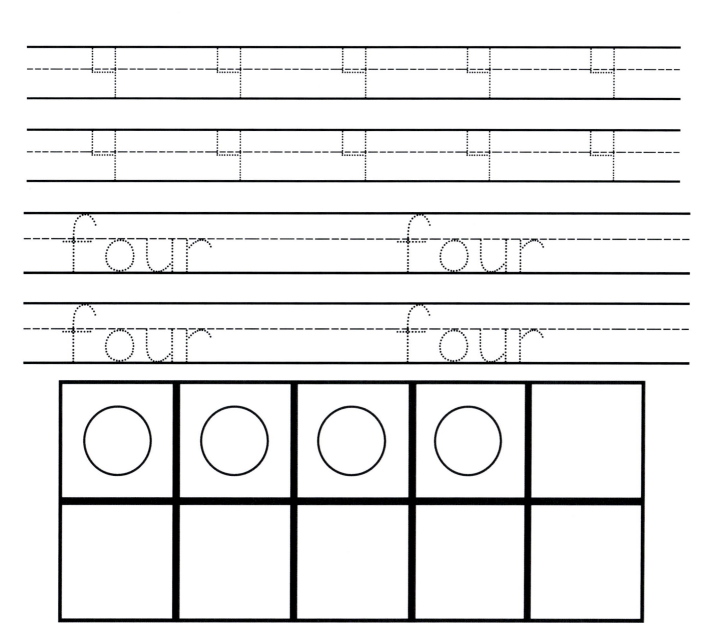

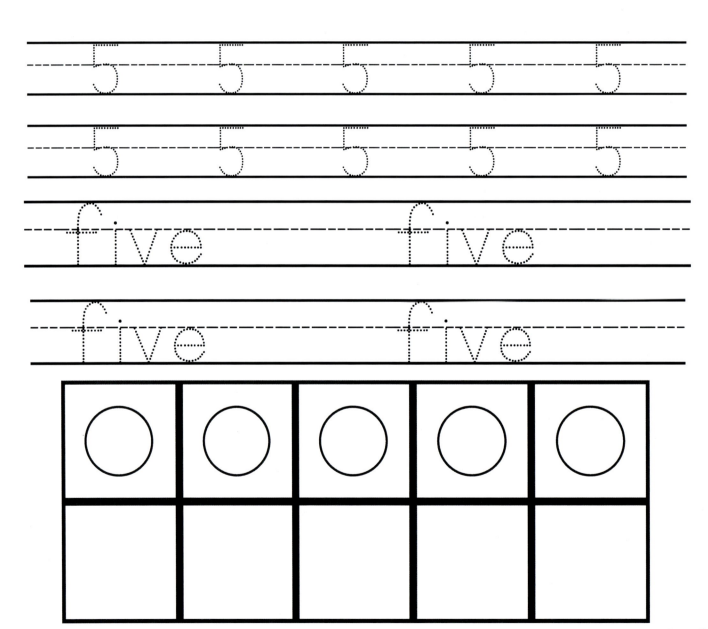

six

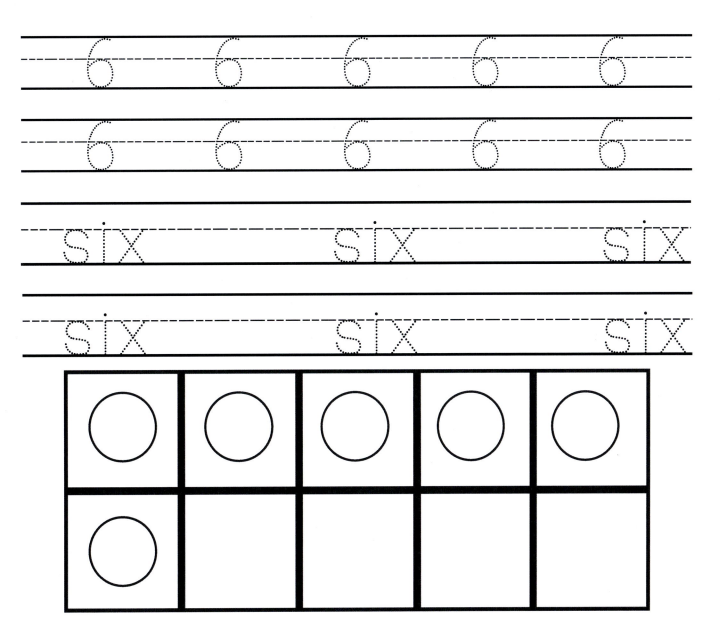

7

seven

7 7 7 7 7

7 7 7 7 7

seven   seven

seven   seven

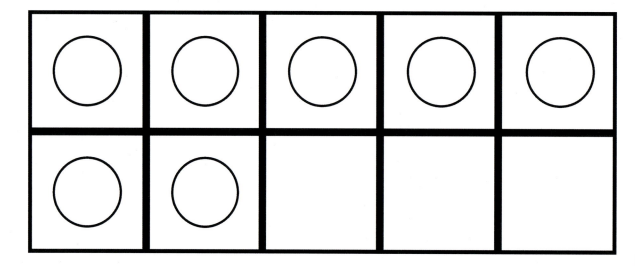

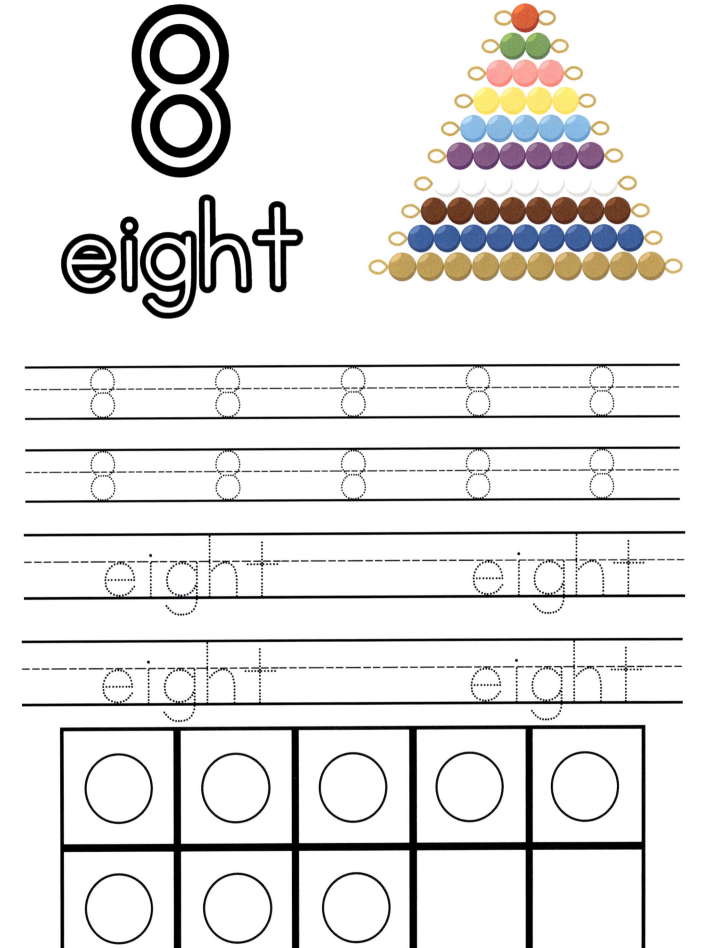

8

eight

nine

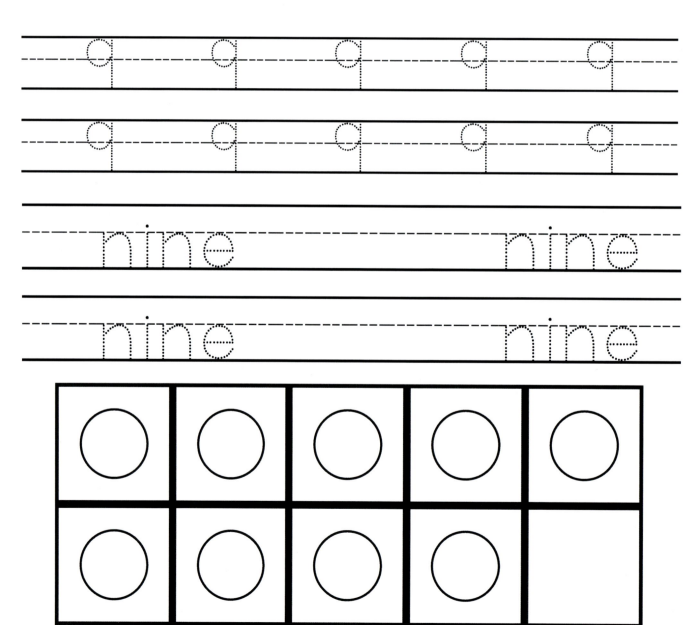

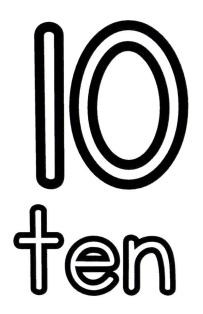

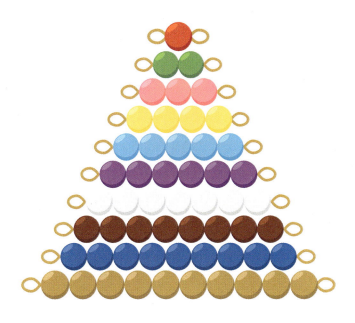

ten

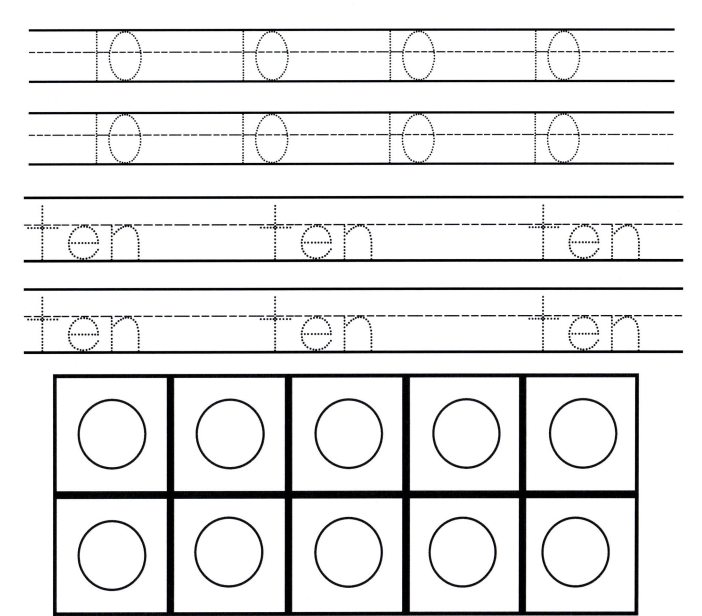

Montessori Short Bead Stairs

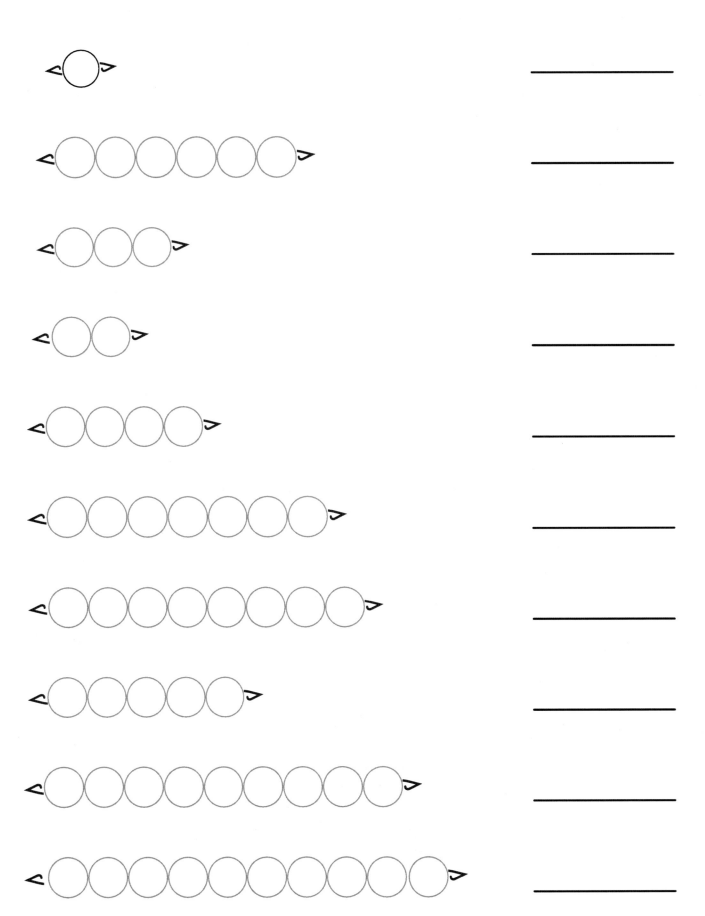

_____

_____

_____

_____

_____

_____

_____

_____

_____

_____

Odd/Even numbers

1 ○	6 ○○○ ○○○
2 ○ ○	7 ○ ○○○ ○○○
3 ○ ○ ○	8 ○○○○ ○○○○
4 ○○ ○○	9 ○ ○○○○ ○○○○
5 ○○ ○ ○○	10 ○○○○○ ○○○○○

Montessori Teen Beads

Use this page with Montessori Teen Board

	10	10	
	11	11	
	12	12	
	13	13	
	14	14	
	15	15	
	16	16	
	17	17	
	18	18	
	19	19	

Page 24-26 to practice with Teen Beads Board

12

11

14

17

18

19

13

16

15

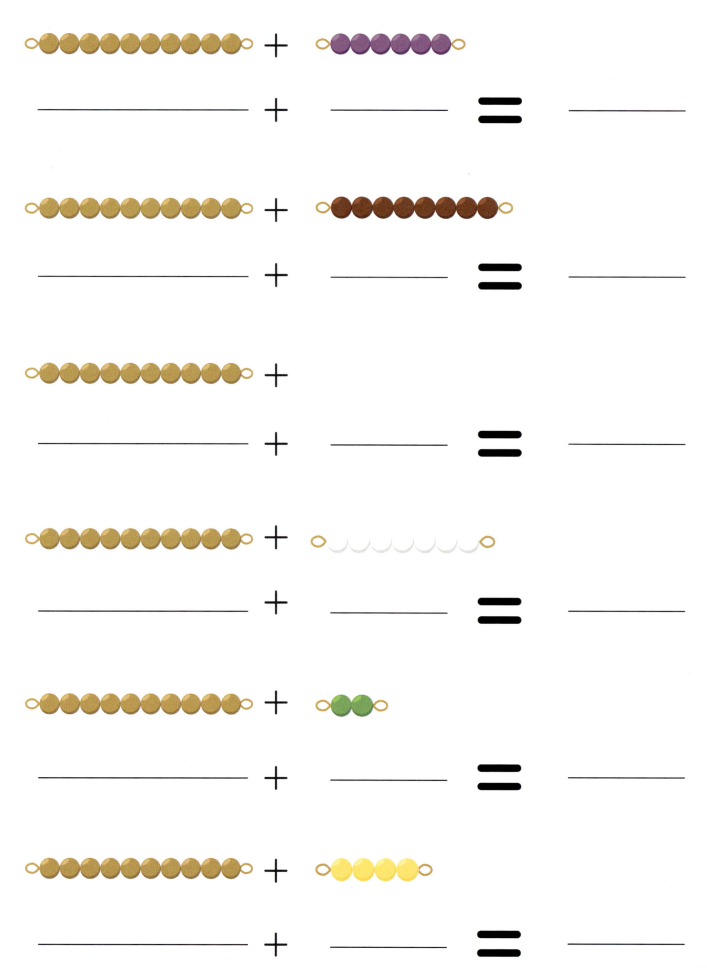

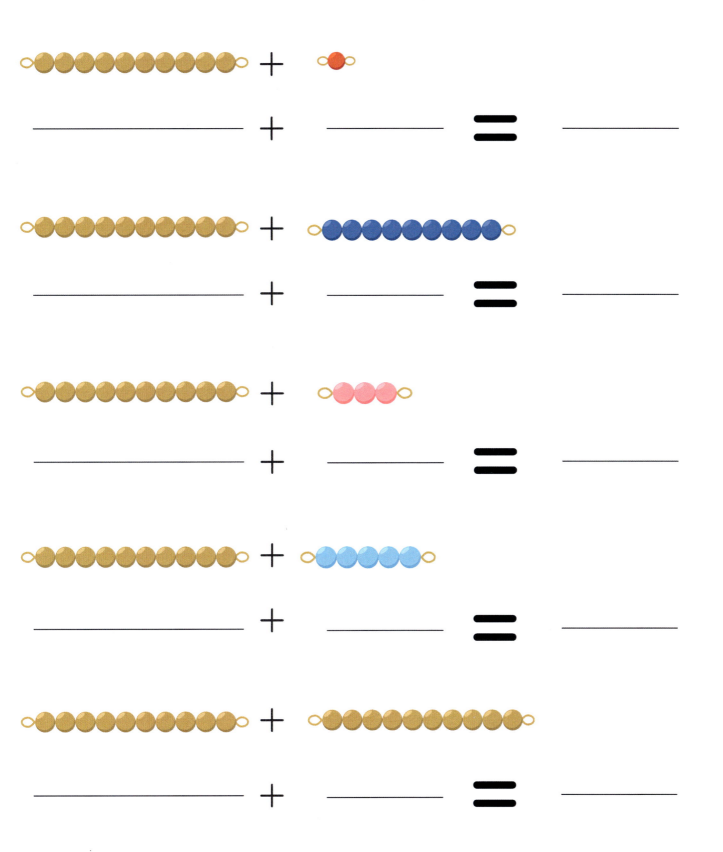

_____ + _____ = _____

_____ + _____ = _____

_____ + _____ = _____

_____ + _____ = _____

_____ + _____ = _____

Cut & Match

thousand	hundred	ten	unit
1000	100	10	I

Golden Beads. Circle the correct number

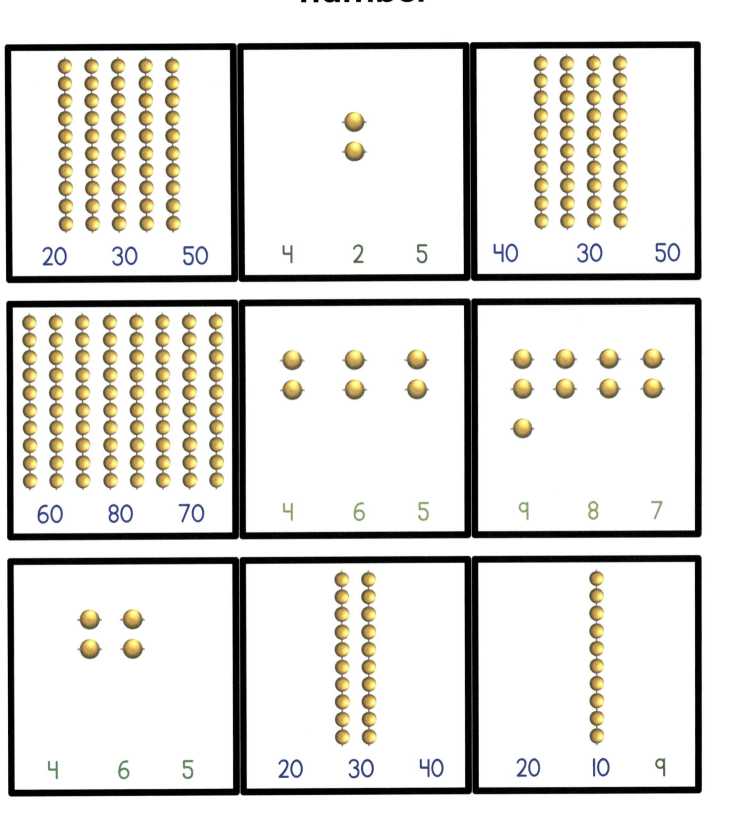

20   30   50

4   2   5

40   30   50

60   80   70

4   6   5

9   8   7

4   6   5

20   30   40

20   10   9

Count by tens and write the number

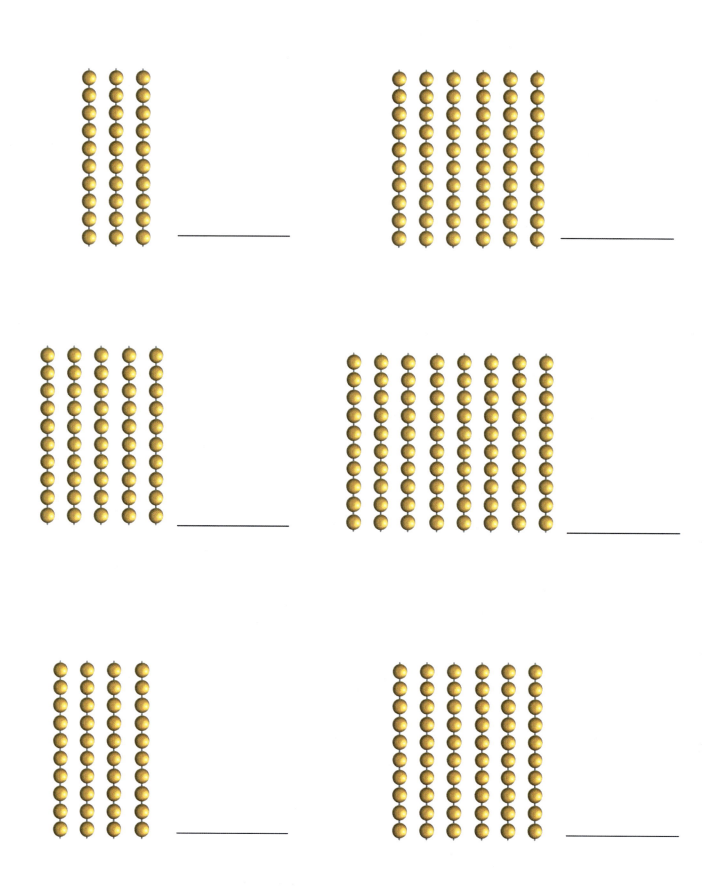

Count by tens and write the number

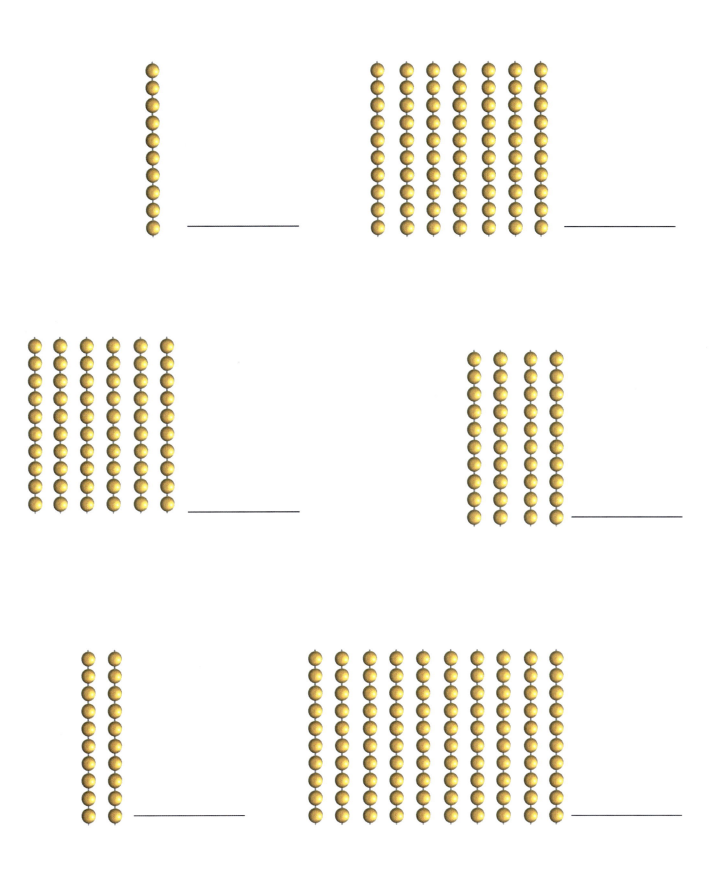

Count the tens and units (ones)

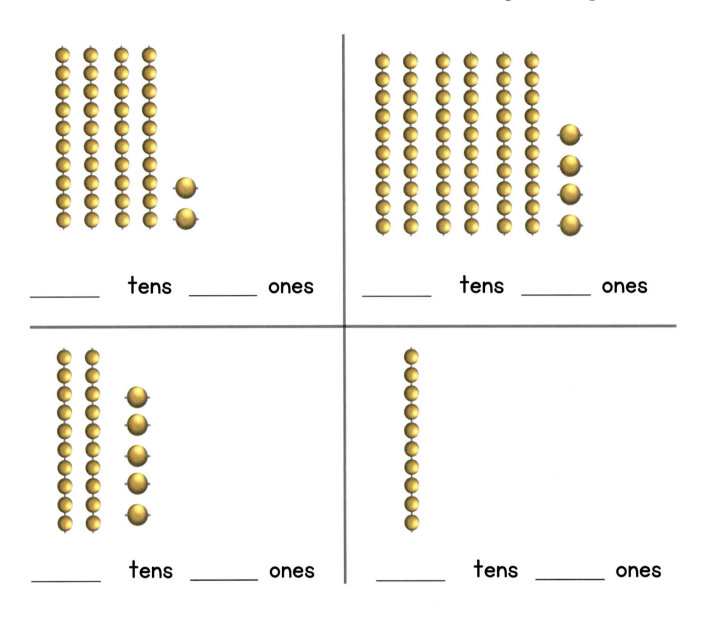

_____ tens _____ ones

_____ tens _____ ones

_____ tens _____ ones

_____ tens _____ ones

⭐ Draw tens bars and units to show the numbers

19

tens	ones/units

Count the tens and units (ones)

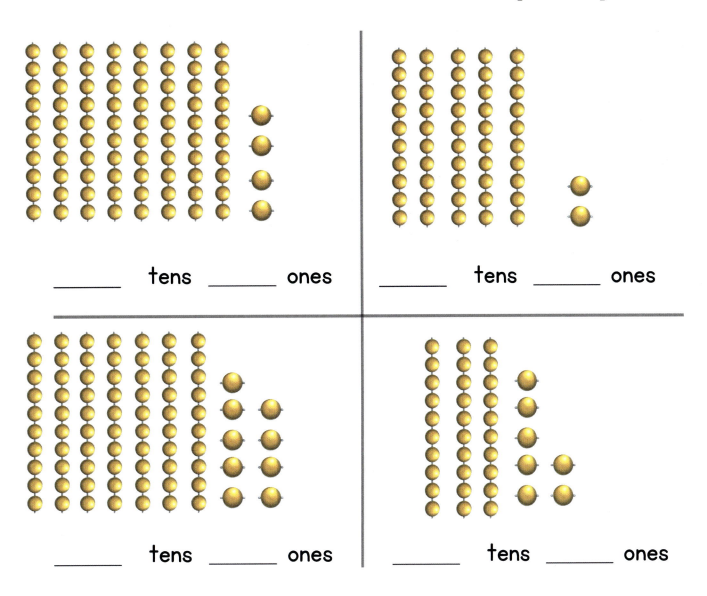

_____ tens _____ ones   _____ tens _____ ones

_____ tens _____ ones   _____ tens _____ ones

⭐ Draw tens bars and units to show the numbers

35	tens	ones/units

Count the tens and units (ones)

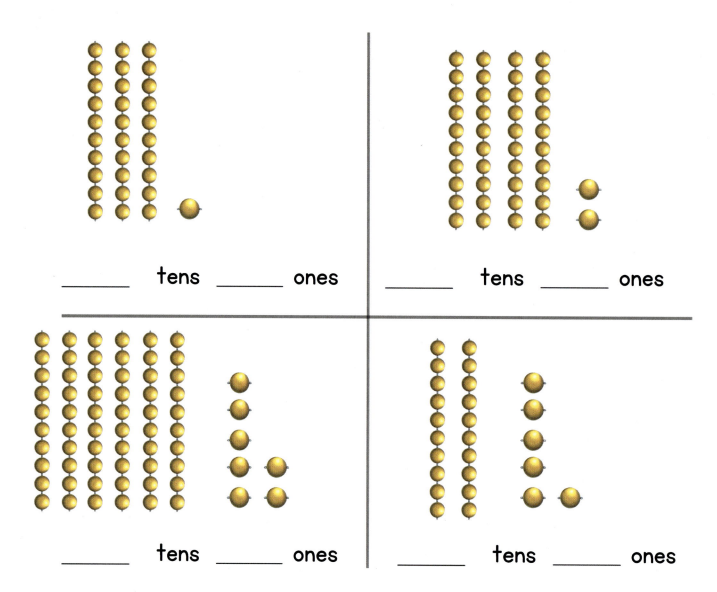

_____ tens _____ ones

_____ tens _____ ones

_____ tens _____ ones

_____ tens _____ ones

⭐ Draw tens bars and units to show the numbers

56

tens	ones/units

Draw tens bars and units to show the numbers

38 ─────── | tens | ones/units

42 ─────── | tens | ones/units

10 ─────── | tens | ones/units

5 ─────── | tens | ones/units

65 ─────── | tens | ones/units

98 ─────── | tens | ones/units

Mat has 59 shells.

_____ tens _____ ones = _____ + _____

Draw tens bars and units to show the numbers

69 ───────── | tens | ones/units

22 ───────── | tens | ones/units

15 ───────── | tens | ones/units

90 ───────── | tens | ones/units

27 ───────── | tens | ones/units

85 ───────── | tens | ones/units

Pam has 44 balloons.

_____ tens _____ ones = _____ + _____

Static addition
Addition Strip Board

5 + 4 = _____   9 + 1 = _____

3 + 2 = _____   5 + 2 = _____

1 + 3 = _____   7 + 2 = _____

8 + 2 = _____   3 + 4 = _____

6 + 1 = _____   2 + 4 = _____

⭐ Write a number sentence (equation)

There are 5 cans of tomato and 2 cans of beans. How many cans in altogether?

_____ + _____ = _____

Static addition
Addition Strip Board

4 + 4 = _____   3 + 4 = _____

3 + 7 = _____   1 + 0 = _____

6 + 3 = _____   6 + 3 = _____

2 + 2 = _____   1 + 4 = _____

5 + 3 = _____   7 + 3 = _____

 Write a number sentence (equation)

There are 7 dolphins swimming in the pod and 3 more join the pod. How many dolphins are in the pod now?

_____ + _____ = _____

Use this with Montessori Large Cards to write numbers

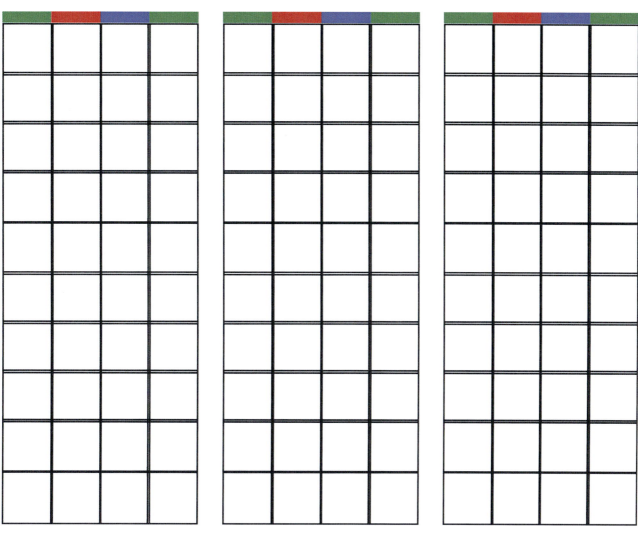

Maya has 4895 pennies.

_____ thousaands _____ hundreds _____ tens _____ ones

Jack has 5081 toys.

_____ thousaands _____ hundreds _____ tens _____ ones

3935

_____ thousaands _____ hundreds _____ tens _____ ones

1744

_____ thousaands _____ hundreds _____ tens _____ ones

4890

_____ thousaands _____ hundreds _____ tens _____ ones

621

_____ thousaands _____ hundreds _____ tens _____ ones

2016

_____ thousaands _____ hundreds _____ tens _____ ones

5409

_____ thousaands _____ hundreds _____ tens _____ ones

Write an expandable form

3935 ＿＿＿ + ＿＿＿ + ＿＿＿ + ＿＿＿

1578 ＿＿＿ + ＿＿＿ + ＿＿＿ + ＿＿＿

4016 ＿＿＿ + ＿＿＿ + ＿＿＿ + ＿＿＿

420 ＿＿＿ + ＿＿＿ + ＿＿＿ + ＿＿＿

7401 ＿＿＿ + ＿＿＿ + ＿＿＿ + ＿＿＿

8149 ＿＿＿ + ＿＿＿ + ＿＿＿ + ＿＿＿

69 ＿＿＿ + ＿＿＿ + ＿＿＿ + ＿＿＿

12 ＿＿＿ + ＿＿＿ + ＿＿＿ + ＿＿＿

100 board chart

1	2	3	4	5	6	7	8	9	10
11	12	13	14	15	16	17	18	19	20
21	22	23	24	25	26	27	28	29	30
31	32	33	34	35	36	37	38	39	40
41	42	43	44	45	46	47	48	49	50
51	52	53	54	55	56	57	58	59	60
61	62	63	64	65	66	67	68	69	70
71	72	73	74	75	76	77	78	79	80
81	82	83	84	85	86	87	88	89	90
91	92	93	94	95	96	97	98	99	100

100 board chart

Static addition (+)
Golden Beads Material

		2	5
		1	4

	2	3	4
	5	5	2

2	2	2	2
2	2	2	2

3	2	4	5
	2	1	1

	7	2	3
9	1	5	2

4	1	3	8
1	7	5	0

	2	2	5
		1	4

		3	4
	5	5	2

2	3	0	1
		9	2

2	1	2	5
2	2	1	4

	2	3	4
	5	5	2

3	4	6	5
1	0	1	3

Static addition (+)
Golden Beads Material

		3	0
	2	5	4

2	1	2	3
	4	5	6

1	0	9	8
4	3	0	1

4	8	3	4
	0	6	1

	4	0	3
1	1	9	3

0	2	3	7
8	2	6	1

	1	3	6
	1	2	2

		1	4
	3	0	5

4	5	0	1
	4	9	2

6	0	3	4
2	3	5	4

	0	9	4
	1	1	1

5	2	7	3
2	4	2	0

Single-digit addition (+)

Use Addition Strip Board for pages 47-53

1	+	0	=	
1	+	1	=	
1	+	2	=	
1	+	3	=	
1	+	4	=	
1	+	5	=	
1	+	6	=	
1	+	7	=	
1	+	8	=	
1	+	9	=	
1	+	10	=	

2	+	0	=	
2	+	1	=	
2	+	2	=	
2	+	3	=	
2	+	4	=	
2	+	5	=	
2	+	6	=	
2	+	7	=	
2	+	8	=	
2	+	9	=	
2	+	10	=	

Single-digit addition (+)

3	+	0	=	
3	+	1	=	
3	+	2	=	
3	+	3	=	
3	+	4	=	
3	+	5	=	
3	+	6	=	
3	+	7	=	
3	+	8	=	
3	+	9	=	
3	+	10	=	

4	+	0	=	
4	+	1	=	
4	+	2	=	
4	+	3	=	
4	+	4	=	
4	+	5	=	
4	+	6	=	
4	+	7	=	
4	+	8	=	
4	+	9	=	
4	+	10	=	

Single-digit addition (+)

5	+	0	=		6	+	0	=	
5	+	1	=		6	+	1	=	
5	+	2	=		6	+	2	=	
5	+	3	=		6	+	3	=	
5	+	4	=		6	+	4	=	
5	+	5	=		6	+	5	=	
5	+	6	=		6	+	6	=	
5	+	7	=		6	+	7	=	
5	+	8	=		6	+	8	=	
5	+	9	=		6	+	9	=	
5	+	10	=		6	+	10	=	

Single-digit addition (+)

7	+	0	=	
7	+	1	=	
7	+	2	=	
7	+	3	=	
7	+	4	=	
7	+	5	=	
7	+	6	=	
7	+	7	=	
7	+	8	=	
7	+	9	=	
7	+	10	=	

8	+	0	=	
8	+	1	=	
8	+	2	=	
8	+	3	=	
8	+	4	=	
8	+	5	=	
8	+	6	=	
8	+	7	=	
8	+	8	=	
8	+	9	=	
8	+	10	=	

Single-digit addition (+)

9	+	0	=	
9	+	1	=	
9	+	2	=	
9	+	3	=	
9	+	4	=	
9	+	5	=	
9	+	6	=	
9	+	7	=	
9	+	8	=	
9	+	9	=	
9	+	10	=	

10	+	0	=	
10	+	1	=	
10	+	2	=	
10	+	3	=	
10	+	4	=	
10	+	5	=	
10	+	6	=	
10	+	7	=	
10	+	8	=	
10	+	9	=	
10	+	10	=	

Single-digit addition (+)

2	+	0	=	
9	+	1	=	
5	+	2	=	
3	+	3	=	
4	+	4	=	
8	+	5	=	
6	+	6	=	
2	+	7	=	
7	+	8	=	
7	+	9	=	
0	+	10	=	

3	+	0	=	
7	+	1	=	
6	+	2	=	
9	+	3	=	
8	+	4	=	
2	+	5	=	
0	+	6	=	
3	+	7	=	
9	+	8	=	
2	+	9	=	
1	+	10	=	

Single-digit addition (+)

5	+	0	=	
2	+	1	=	
6	+	2	=	
7	+	3	=	
9	+	4	=	
6	+	5	=	
4	+	6	=	
1	+	7	=	
0	+	8	=	
8	+	9	=	
1	+	10	=	

0	+	0	=	
6	+	1	=	
4	+	2	=	
8	+	3	=	
0	+	4	=	
8	+	5	=	
6	+	6	=	
7	+	7	=	
5	+	8	=	
3	+	9	=	
2	+	10	=	

Algebra: Use symbols to compare.
Write <, >, or =

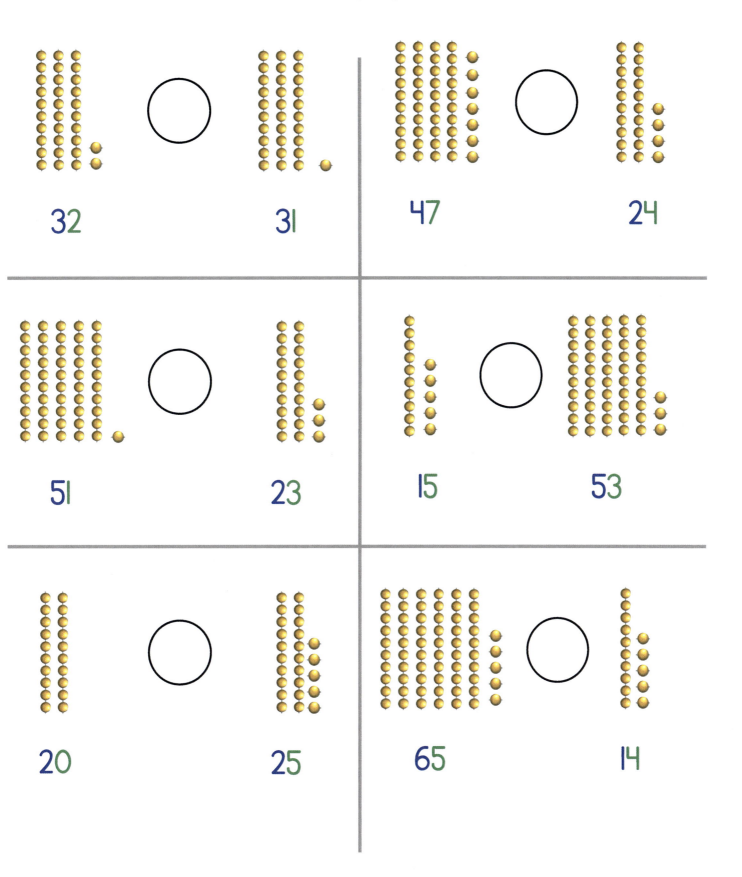

32 ◯ 31

47 ◯ 24

51 ◯ 23

15 ◯ 53

20 ◯ 25

65 ◯ 14

Algebra: Use symbols to compare.
Write <, >, or =

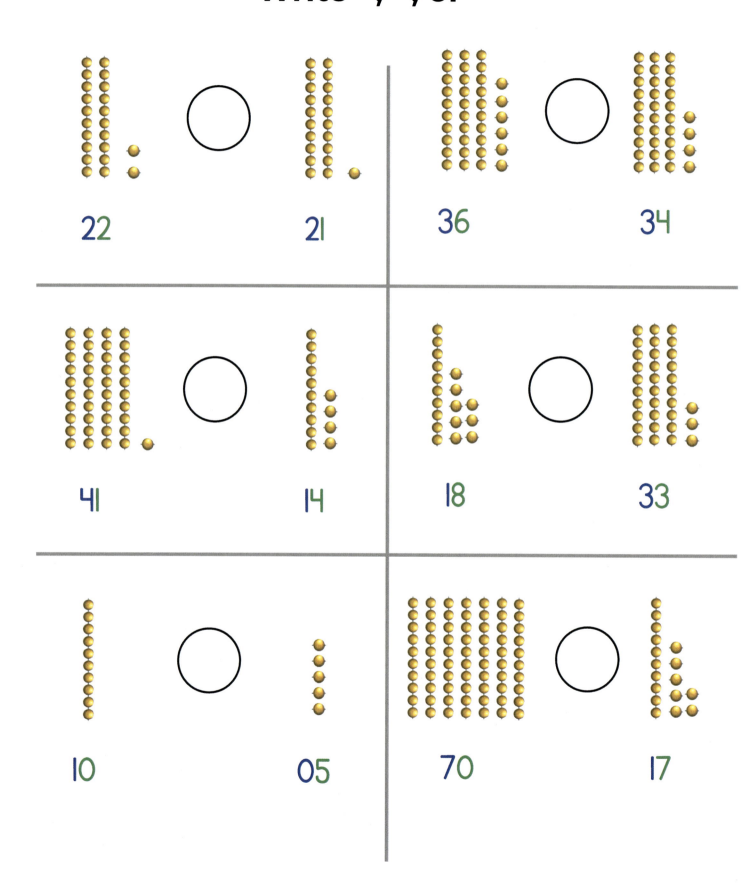

22　○　21

36　○　34

41　○　14

18　○　33

10　○　05

70　○　17

Positive Snake Game

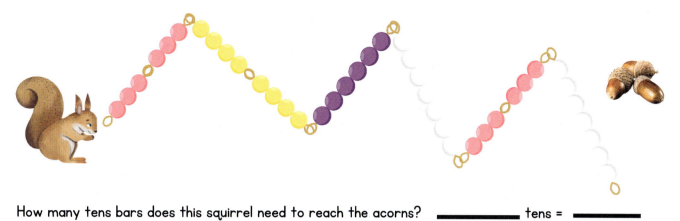

How many tens bars does this squirrel need to reach the acorns? _____ tens = _____

How many tens bars does this squirrel need to reach the acorns? _____ tens = _____

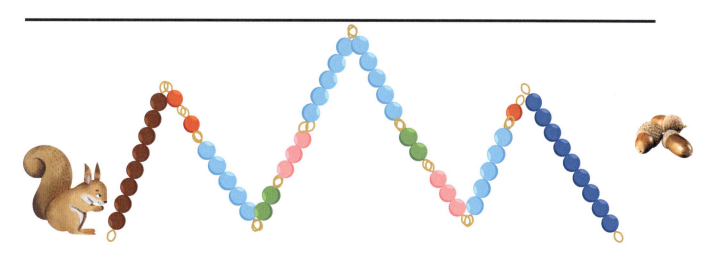

How many tens bars does this squirrel need to get to the acorns? _____ tens = _____

Positive Snake Game

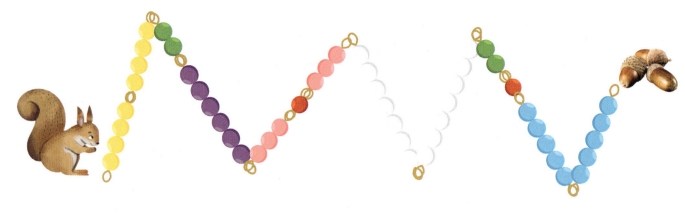

How many tens bars does this squirrel need to reach the acorns? _____ tens = _____

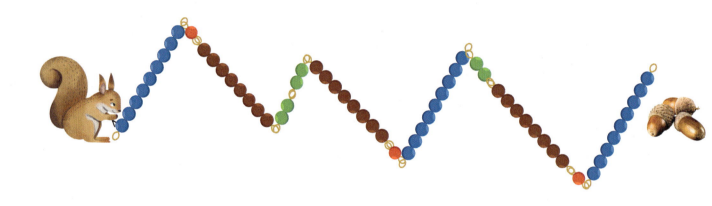

How many tens bars does this squirrel need to reach the acorns? _____ tens = _____

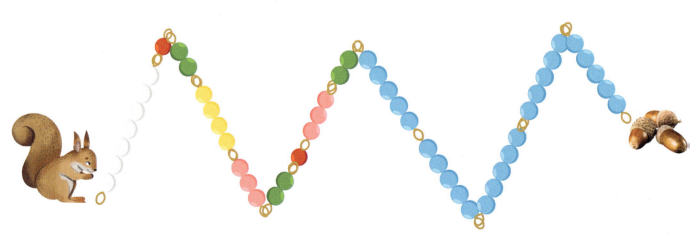

How many tens bars does this squirrel need to get to the acorns? _____ tens = _____

Single-digit multiplication (x)

Use Multiplication Bead Board for pages 58-64

1	✕	0	=	
1	✕	1	=	
1	✕	2	=	
1	✕	3	=	
1	✕	4	=	
1	✕	5	=	
1	✕	6	=	
1	✕	7	=	
1	✕	8	=	
1	✕	9	=	
1	✕	10	=	

2	✕	0	=	
2	✕	1	=	
2	✕	2	=	
2	✕	3	=	
2	✕	4	=	
2	✕	5	=	
2	✕	6	=	
2	✕	7	=	
2	✕	8	=	
2	✕	9	=	
2	✕	10	=	

Single-digit multiplication (x)

3	✖	0	▬	
3	✖	1	▬	
3	✖	2	▬	
3	✖	3	▬	
3	✖	4	▬	
3	✖	5	▬	
3	✖	6	▬	
3	✖	7	▬	
3	✖	8	▬	
3	✖	9	▬	
3	✖	10	▬	

4	✖	0	▬	
4	✖	1	▬	
4	✖	2	▬	
4	✖	3	▬	
4	✖	4	▬	
4	✖	5	▬	
4	✖	6	▬	
4	✖	7	▬	
4	✖	8	▬	
4	✖	9	▬	
4	✖	10	▬	

Single-digit multiplication (x)

5	✖	0	=	
5	✖	1	=	
5	✖	2	=	
5	✖	3	=	
5	✖	4	=	
5	✖	5	=	
5	✖	6	=	
5	✖	7	=	
5	✖	8	=	
5	✖	9	=	
5	✖	10	=	

6	✖	0	=	
6	✖	1	=	
6	✖	2	=	
6	✖	3	=	
6	✖	4	=	
6	✖	5	=	
6	✖	6	=	
6	✖	7	=	
6	✖	8	=	
6	✖	9	=	
6	✖	10	=	

Single-digit multiplication (x)

7	✕	0	=	
7	✕	1	=	
7	✕	2	=	
7	✕	3	=	
7	✕	4	=	
7	✕	5	=	
7	✕	6	=	
7	✕	7	=	
7	✕	8	=	
7	✕	9	=	
7	✕	10	=	

8	✕	0	=	
8	✕	1	=	
8	✕	2	=	
8	✕	3	=	
8	✕	4	=	
8	✕	5	=	
8	✕	6	=	
8	✕	7	=	
8	✕	8	=	
8	✕	9	=	
8	✕	10	=	

Single-digit multiplication (x)

9	✖	0	=	
9	✖	1	=	
9	✖	2	=	
9	✖	3	=	
9	✖	4	=	
9	✖	5	=	
9	✖	6	=	
9	✖	7	=	
9	✖	8	=	
9	✖	9	=	
9	✖	10	=	

10	✖	0	=	
10	✖	1	=	
10	✖	2	=	
10	✖	3	=	
10	✖	4	=	
10	✖	5	=	
10	✖	6	=	
10	✖	7	=	
10	✖	8	=	
10	✖	9	=	
10	✖	10	=	

Single-digit multiplication (x)

10	✕	0	=	
9	✕	1	=	
8	✕	2	=	
3	✕	3	=	
4	✕	4	=	
1	✕	5	=	
6	✕	6	=	
4	✕	7	=	
3	✕	8	=	
7	✕	9	=	
5	✕	10	=	

3	✕	0	=	
7	✕	1	=	
6	✕	2	=	
9	✕	3	=	
8	✕	4	=	
2	✕	5	=	
0	✕	6	=	
3	✕	7	=	
9	✕	8	=	
2	✕	9	=	
1	✕	10	=	

Single-digit multiplication (x)

2	✗	4	=	
6	✗	2	=	
3	✗	6	=	
3	✗	5	=	
4	✗	4	=	
9	✗	7	=	
5	✗	10	=	
7	✗	7	=	
2	✗	1	=	
3	✗	9	=	
4	✗	8	=	

5	✗	0	=	
9	✗	1	=	
7	✗	2	=	
3	✗	3	=	
1	✗	4	=	
5	✗	5	=	
8	✗	6	=	
2	✗	7	=	
10	✗	8	=	
4	✗	9	=	
6	✗	10	=	

Counting 1 to 100

Fill in the missing numbers.

1	2	3	4		6	7	8	9	10
11	12	13	14	15	16	17		19	20
21		23	24	25		27	28	29	30
31	32	33		35	36	37	38	39	40
41	42	43	44		46	47	48		50
51		53	54	55	56	57	58	59	
61	62	63	64		66		68	69	70
	72	73		75	76	77	78		80
81	82		84	85		87		89	90
	92	93	94	95	96		98	99	

Count forward or backward. Write the numbers

44, 45, ___ , ___ , ___ , ___ , ___

19, 18, ___ , ___ , ___ , ___ , ___

25, 26, ___ , ___ , ___ , ___ , ___

 Skip count. Write the missing numbers.

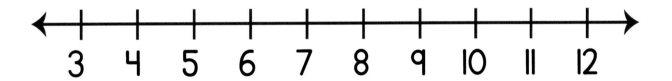

3, 6, ___ , ___ ,

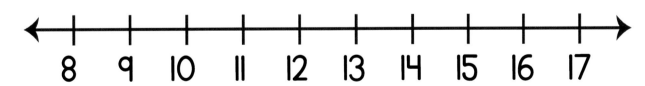

4, 8, ___ , ___ ,

Count forward or backward. Write the numbers

92, 91, ___ , ___ , ___ , ___ , ___

57, 58, ___ , ___ , ___ , ___ , ___

31, 30, ___ , ___ , ___ , ___ , ___

 Skip count. Write the missing numbers.

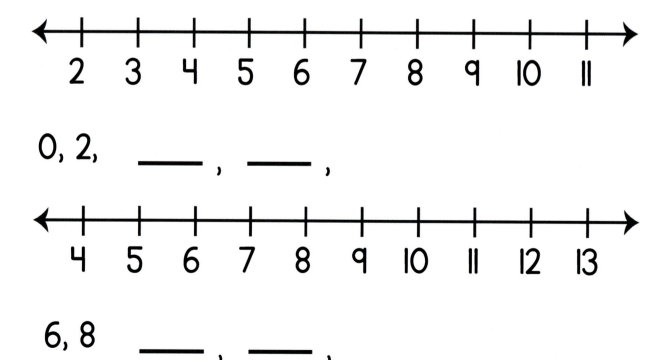

0, 2, ___ , ___ ,

6, 8 ___ , ___ ,

Write the missing numbers

10, 20, ___, ___, 30, ___, ___, ___

5, ___, 15, 20, ___, ___, 35, ___

31, 30, ___, ___, ___, ___, ___

5, 6, ___, 8, ___, ___, ___

2, ___, 6, ___, ___, 12, ___

15, 14, ___, ___, ___, ___, ___

88, 89, ___, ___, ___, ___, ___

0, 4, ___, ___, ___, ___, ___

Static multiplication (x)
Golden Beads Material

		1	2
			2

	2	3	4
			2

2	2	2	2
			3

3	2	4	5
			1

	1	2	3
			3

	1	1	2
			4

	2	2	3
			3

		3	4
			0

2	3	0	1
			3

	1	2	1
			4

	2	3	3
			2

3	4	6	5
			1

Solve the equation with Positive Snake Game

Problem:

$$5 + 6 + 7 + 9 + 5 + 8 + 4 + 3 + 7 + 8 + 4 + 3 + 2$$

Answer: tens = _____   units= _____   = _____

Problem:

$$7 + 9 + 5 + 9 + 5 + 6 + 6 + 3 + 9 + 8 + 5 + 3 + 6$$

Answer: tens = _____   units= _____   = _____

Problem:

$$1 + 9 + 6 + 8 + 7 + 9 + 6 + 4 + 7 + 9 + 8 + 7 + 2$$

Answer: tens = _____   units= _____   = _____

Solve the equation with Positive Snake Game

Problem:

$$4 + 4 + 3 + 6 + 5 + 9 + 7 + 6 + 4 + 8 + 7 + 6 + 1$$

Answer: tens = _____   units= _____   = _____

Problem:

$$6 + 6 + 4 + 3 + 8 + 7 + 6 + 4 + 6 + 7 + 9 + 1 + 2$$

Answer: tens = _____   units= _____   = _____

Problem:

$$1 + 9 + 6 + 8 + 7 + 9 + 6 + 4 + 7 + 9 + 8 + 7 + 2$$

Answer: tens = _____   units= _____   = _____

Single-digit subtraction (-)
Use Subtraction Strip Board for pages 72-77

10	—	0	=	
10	—	1	=	
10	—	2	=	
10	—	3	=	
10	—	4	=	
10	—	5	=	
10	—	6	=	
10	—	7	=	
10	—	8	=	
10	—	9	=	
10	—	10	=	

9	—	0	=	
9	—	1	=	
9	—	2	=	
9	—	3	=	
9	—	4	=	
9	—	5	=	
9	—	6	=	
9	—	7	=	
9	—	8	=	
9	—	9	=	

Single-digit subtraction (-)

8	−	0	=	
8	−	1	=	
8	−	2	=	
8	−	3	=	
8	−	4	=	
8	−	5	=	
8	−	6	=	
8	−	7	=	
8	−	8	=	

7	−	0	=	
7	−	1	=	
7	−	2	=	
7	−	3	=	
7	−	4	=	
7	−	5	=	
7	−	6	=	
7	−	7	=	

Single-digit subtraction (-)

6	—	0	=	
6	—	1	=	
6	—	2	=	
6	—	3	=	
6	—	4	=	
6	—	5	=	
6	—	6	=	

5	—	0	=	
5	—	1	=	
5	—	2	=	
5	—	3	=	
5	—	4	=	
5	—	5	=	

4	—	0	=	
4	—	1	=	
4	—	2	=	
4	—	3	=	
4	—	4	=	

Single-digit subtraction (-)

3	—	0	=	
3	—	1	=	
3	—	2	=	
3	—	3	=	

2	—	0	=	
2	—	1	=	
2	—	2	=	

1	—	0	=	
1	—	1	=	

Single-digit subtraction (-)

8	—	6	=	
4	—	1	=	
7	—	2	=	
9	—	5	=	
10	—	4	=	
6	—	3	=	
6	—	6	=	
9	—	7	=	
10	—	2	=	
5	—	2	=	
10	—	10	=	

4	—	0	=	
3	—	1	=	
10	—	6	=	
7	—	3	=	
5	—	4	=	
9	—	2	=	
8	—	6	=	
3	—	1	=	
8	—	8	=	
9	—	4	=	
2	—	0	=	

Single-digit subtraction (-)

4	—	3	=	
9	—	1	=	
8	—	2	=	
5	—	5	=	
7	—	4	=	
8	—	3	=	
9	—	6	=	
8	—	7	=	
5	—	2	=	
4	—	2	=	
10	—	0	=	

6	—	0	=	
10	—	1	=	
8	—	6	=	
8	—	3	=	
9	—	4	=	
7	—	2	=	
6	—	6	=	
5	—	1	=	
9	—	8	=	
4	—	4	=	
3	—	0	=	

Mental Math

Learning goal: Practice your mental arithmetic skills.

13 - 7 =

21 - 2 =

16 - 11 =

10 - 7 =

15 - 9 =

27 - 11 =

13 - 8 =

21 - 11 =

25 - 19 =

12 - 7 =

23 - 8 =

12 + 5 =

12 + 13 =

11 + 9 =

3 + 18 =

23 + 15 =

7 + 15 =

31 + 4 =

15 + 7 =

32 + 7 =

13 + 9 =

3 + 26 =

13 + 9 =

22 - 7 =

16 + 8 =

15 - 6 =

12 + 19 =

22 - 5 =

23 + 4 =

11 - 7 =

22 + 9 =

22 - 4 =

23 + 6 =

Addition/Subtraction word problems

Learning goal: Practice your mental arithmetic skills.

1. Albie has 11 toy cars and he left four at the park. How many cars does he have now?

2. Ally, Ollie and Henry each eat six grapes. How many grapes did they eat in total?

3. Finley read 11 pages yesterday and eight today. How many pages did he read altogether?

4. Joey ate three chocolates, four lollipops and six pieces of candy. How much did he eat in total?

5. Carlos had 16 balloons. Two popped and six blew away. How many does he have left now?

6. Kara has 20 pet frogs. One died and four jumped away. How many does she have left?

Static subtraction (-)
Golden Beads Material

		5	6
		2	4

4	7	8	9
	4	5	6

7	7	9	8
4	3	0	1

4	8	6	4
	0	6	1

	4	9	3
	1	0	3

8	2	8	7
8	2	6	1

	1	3	6
	1	2	2

		9	9
	0	5	5

4	5	2	6
	4	0	1

6	4	6	4
2	3	5	4

	8	9	4
	1	1	1

5	6	7	3
2	4	2	0

Static subtraction (-)
Golden Beads Material

		7	6
		3	2

5	6	4	9
	4	2	3

9	8	9	5
1	2	6	4

3	4	7	8
	3	5	1

	7	9	3
	2	2	1

8	7	5	4
2	2	4	2

	6	4	2
	1	1	0

		4	9
		2	3

6	3	1	7
	2	0	5

7	9	6	8
4	3	2	4

	9	9	7
	6	1	1

9	8	7	3
2	4	3	1

Subtraction word problems

There are 13 bugs. 6 are tiny. The rest are big. How many bugs are big?

$13 - \boxed{} = 6$

_____ bugs are big

---

14 seals are on the ice. Some swim away. There are 7 seals left on the ice. How many swim away?

$14 - \boxed{} = 7$

_____ seals swim away

---

9 cows are in the barn. Some go outside. There are 4 cows left in the barn. How many go outside?

$9 - \boxed{} = 4$

_____ cows go outside

Subtraction word problems

Kim has 12 pennies. She gives some away. Now she has 7 pennies. How many pennies does she have now?

$12 - \boxed{} = 7$

Kim gave away _____ pennies.

---

10 horses are on the field. Some go back to the barn. There are 7 horses left on the field. How many are in the barn?

$10 - \boxed{} = 7$

_____ horses in the barn.

Sam has 15 balloons. He gives some to his friend. Now he has 8 balloons. How many did he give to his friend?

$15 - \boxed{} = 8$

Sam gave away _____ balloons.

Single-digit division (÷)

Use Division Bead Board for pages 84 - 89

1	÷	1	=	
2	÷	1	=	
3	÷	1	=	
4	÷	1	=	
5	÷	1	=	
6	÷	1	=	
7	÷	1	=	
8	÷	1	=	
9	÷	1	=	
10	÷	1	=	
0	÷	1	=	

0	÷	2	=	
2	÷	2	=	
4	÷	2	=	
6	÷	2	=	
8	÷	2	=	
10	÷	2	=	
12	÷	2	=	
14	÷	2	=	
16	÷	2	=	
18	÷	2	=	
20	÷	2	=	

Single-digit division (÷)

0	÷	3	=	
3	÷	3	=	
6	÷	3	=	
9	÷	3	=	
12	÷	3	=	
15	÷	3	=	
18	÷	3	=	
21	÷	3	=	
24	÷	3	=	
27	÷	3	=	
30	÷	3	=	

0	÷	4	=	
4	÷	4	=	
8	÷	4	=	
12	÷	4	=	
16	÷	4	=	
20	÷	4	=	
24	÷	4	=	
28	÷	4	=	
32	÷	4	=	
36	÷	4	=	
40	÷	4	=	

Single-digit division (÷)

0	÷	5	=	
5	÷	5	=	
10	÷	5	=	
15	÷	5	=	
20	÷	5	=	
25	÷	5	=	
30	÷	5	=	
35	÷	5	=	
40	÷	5	=	
45	÷	5	=	
50	÷	5	=	

0	÷	6	=	
6	÷	6	=	
12	÷	6	=	
18	÷	6	=	
24	÷	6	=	
30	÷	6	=	
36	÷	6	=	
42	÷	6	=	
48	÷	6	=	
54	÷	6	=	
60	÷	6	=	

Single-digit division (÷)

0	÷	7	=	
7	÷	7	=	
14	÷	7	=	
21	÷	7	=	
28	÷	7	=	
35	÷	7	=	
42	÷	7	=	
49	÷	7	=	
56	÷	7	=	
63	÷	7	=	
70	÷	7	=	

0	÷	8	=	
8	÷	8	=	
16	÷	8	=	
24	÷	8	=	
32	÷	8	=	
40	÷	8	=	
48	÷	8	=	
56	÷	8	=	
64	÷	8	=	
72	÷	8	=	
80	÷	8	=	

Single-digit division (÷)

0	÷	9	=	
9	÷	9	=	
18	÷	9	=	
27	÷	9	=	
36	÷	9	=	
45	÷	9	=	
54	÷	9	=	
63	÷	9	=	
72	÷	9	=	
81	÷	9	=	
90	÷	9	=	

0	÷	10	=	
10	÷	10	=	
20	÷	10	=	
30	÷	10	=	
40	÷	10	=	
50	÷	10	=	
60	÷	10	=	
70	÷	10	=	
80	÷	10	=	
90	÷	10	=	
100	÷	10	=	

Single-digit division (÷)

12	÷	2	=	
20	÷	5	=	
4	÷	4	=	
16	÷	2	=	
12	÷	3	=	
10	÷	5	=	
0	÷	9	=	
14	÷	7	=	
6	÷	3	=	
18	÷	9	=	
36	÷	6	=	

16	÷	8	=	
49	÷	7	=	
9	÷	3	=	
72	÷	9	=	
64	÷	8	=	
28	÷	7	=	
30	÷	6	=	
20	÷	4	=	
50	÷	5	=	
35	÷	7	=	
18	÷	2	=	

Numbers to 20 addition

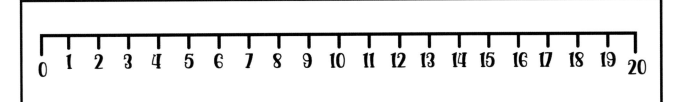

11 + 5 = _____   17 + 2 = _____   12 + 4 = _____

4 + 13 = _____   5 + 14 = _____   8 + 10 = _____

16 + 8 = _____   9 + 2 = _____   10 + 3 = _____

9 + 13 = _____   11 + 6 = _____   11 + 9 = _____

12 + 7 = _____   15 + 4 = _____   14 + 0 = _____

4 + 12 = _____   2 + 15 = _____   13 + 5 = _____

10 + 9 = _____   1 + 18 = _____   20 + 0 = _____

8 + 12 = _____   14 + 6 = _____   5 + 6 = _____

12 + 5 = _____   12 + 0 = _____   7 + 4 = _____

7 + 8 = _____   2 + 14 = _____   7 + 6 = _____

11 + 6 = _____   10 + 10 = _____   9 + 5 = _____

1 + 12 = _____   1 + 19 = _____   3 + 9 = _____

0 + 13 = _____   3 + 12 = _____   4 + 6 = _____

9 + 7 = _____   7 + 13 = _____   4 + 9 = _____

9 + 11 = _____   9 + 10 = _____   13 + 5 = _____

Static division (÷)
Golden Beads Material

		3	6
			3

2	6	4	2
			2

4	8	8	4
			4

9	6	9	3
			3

		9	3
			3

8	4	4	4
			2

	8	4	2
			4

		6	9
			3

5	5	0	5
			5

7	9	6	8
			1

	9	9	6
			3

4	8	0	6
			2

Order the numbers from smallest to largest

| 46 | 170 | 107 | 16 | 73 |

[ ] < [ ] < [ ] < [ ] < [ ]

Fill in the missing numbers below

➡ | 19 | 20 | [ ] | [ ] | 23 | [ ] | 25 |

➡ | 78 | 77 | [ ] | 75 | [ ] | [ ] | 72 |

➡ | 99 | 100 | [ ] | 102 | [ ] | [ ] | [ ] |

Circle the larger number in each pair

| 209   211 | 85   19 | 111   98 |

| 25   52 | 59   79 | 212   213 |

| 36   136 | 144   200 | 422   123 |

| 72   12 | 75   55 | 200   199 |

Multiplication/Division word problems

1   You have 7 boxes of chocolates, and each box contains 6 chocolates each. How many chocolates do you have in total?

2   You decide to buy 3 more boxes of chocolates, again with 6 chocolates inside each box. How many additional chocolates do you have now? How many in total?

3   Your little brother steals 9 of your chocolates. How many chocolates remain?

4   You decide to evenly share the remaining chocolates between your two parents and yourself. How many chocolates will each of you receive?

5   Your brother returns 5 of the chocolates he took. How many chocolates do you have in total now?

Dynamic addition (+)

Use Stamp Game or Golden Beads to exchange and regroup

		3	7
	6	9	4

9	1	9	6
	7	5	6

3	7	4	8
4	3	8	9

5	8	3	4
	6	4	7

	4	9	5
8	7	4	3

0	9	9	7
8	2	6	8

	9	4	6
	3	6	2

		5	6
	9	9	5

6	5	4	1
		4	9	6

6	9	6	4
2	4	7	7

	9	9	4
	6	5	1

7	8	6	9
2	4	8	9

Dynamic addition (+)

Use Stamp Game or Golden Beads to exchange and regroup

1.

		7	9
	9	9	5

2.

8	9	4	6
	7	5	7

3.

4	8	7	8
3	9	8	5

4.

6	8	6	5
	5	7	1

5.

	9	0	5
6	0	6	5

6.

6	9	5	6
2	7	7	8

7.

	4	6	8
	5	6	9

8.

		1	6
	8	2	7

9.

5	9	8	7
	6	2	5

10.

9	9	0	9
0	7	4	5

11.

	6	2	6
	5	8	7

12.

6	9	8	5
1	9	3	4

Use Multiplication Bead Board or Decanomial Bead Bars to solve these problems

$$
\begin{array}{r}2\\ \times\,5\\ \hline\end{array}\qquad
\begin{array}{r}8\\ \times\,6\\ \hline\end{array}\qquad
\begin{array}{r}6\\ \times\,1\\ \hline\end{array}\qquad
\begin{array}{r}4\\ \times\,7\\ \hline\end{array}\qquad
\begin{array}{r}1\\ \times\,3\\ \hline\end{array}\qquad
\begin{array}{r}4\\ \times\,3\\ \hline\end{array}
$$

$$
\begin{array}{r}4\\ \times\,6\\ \hline\end{array}\qquad
\begin{array}{r}6\\ \times\,5\\ \hline\end{array}\qquad
\begin{array}{r}1\\ \times\,6\\ \hline\end{array}\qquad
\begin{array}{r}2\\ \times\,2\\ \hline\end{array}\qquad
\begin{array}{r}3\\ \times\,5\\ \hline\end{array}\qquad
\begin{array}{r}9\\ \times\,4\\ \hline\end{array}
$$

$$
\begin{array}{r}9\\ \times\,6\\ \hline\end{array}\qquad
\begin{array}{r}6\\ \times\,6\\ \hline\end{array}\qquad
\begin{array}{r}8\\ \times\,5\\ \hline\end{array}\qquad
\begin{array}{r}7\\ \times\,5\\ \hline\end{array}\qquad
\begin{array}{r}0\\ \times\,3\\ \hline\end{array}\qquad
\begin{array}{r}8\\ \times\,4\\ \hline\end{array}
$$

$$
\begin{array}{r}5\\ \times\,4\\ \hline\end{array}\qquad
\begin{array}{r}4\\ \times\,6\\ \hline\end{array}\qquad
\begin{array}{r}1\\ \times\,5\\ \hline\end{array}\qquad
\begin{array}{r}4\\ \times\,5\\ \hline\end{array}\qquad
\begin{array}{r}9\\ \times\,1\\ \hline\end{array}\qquad
\begin{array}{r}6\\ \times\,7\\ \hline\end{array}
$$

$$
\begin{array}{r}1\\ \times\,7\\ \hline\end{array}\qquad
\begin{array}{r}0\\ \times\,5\\ \hline\end{array}\qquad
\begin{array}{r}8\\ \times\,6\\ \hline\end{array}\qquad
\begin{array}{r}7\\ \times\,6\\ \hline\end{array}\qquad
\begin{array}{r}4\\ \times\,5\\ \hline\end{array}\qquad
\begin{array}{r}2\\ \times\,6\\ \hline\end{array}
$$

Math facts. Solve & write the equations

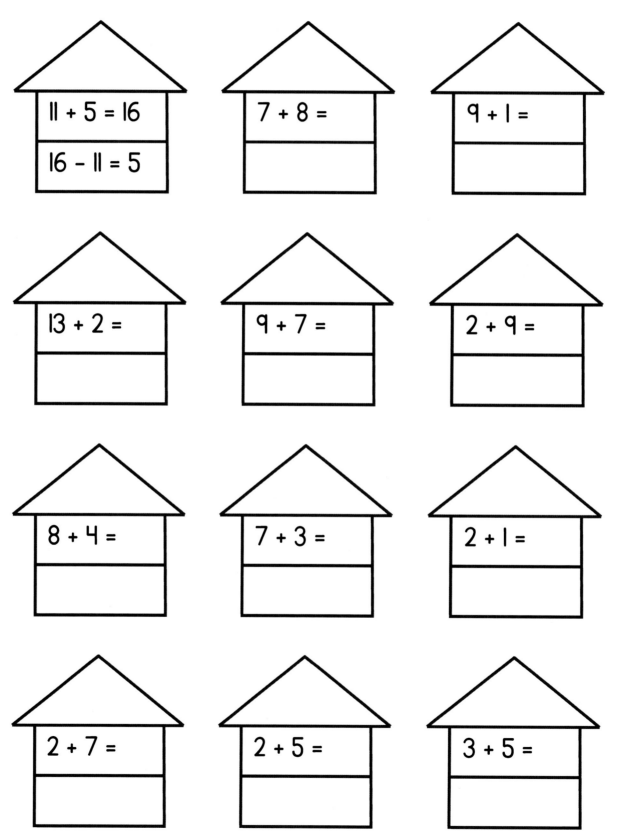

11 + 5 = 16
16 − 11 = 5

7 + 8 =

9 + 1 =

13 + 2 =

9 + 7 =

2 + 9 =

8 + 4 =

7 + 3 =

2 + 1 =

2 + 7 =

2 + 5 =

3 + 5 =

Dynamic multiplication (x)

Use Stamp Game or Golden Beads to exchange and regroup

		7	3
			4

	1	3	5
			2

1	4	3	4
			3

1	5	4	3
			5

	1	2	2
			6

	1	7	3
			4

	2	2	3
			5

		8	5
			2

1	9	2	4
			3

	1	8	3
			4

	2	3	3
			6

1	4	2	5
			4

Dynamic multiplication (x)

Use Stamp Game or Golden Beads to exchange and regroup

	7	7	2
			2

1	4	3	5
			3

1	2	2	4
			5

1	2	0	6
			4

	5	1	1
			4

	2	7	3
			2

		2	3
			9

		4	3
			5

1	0	2	2
			6

	1	2	1
			8

	2	1	3
			7

1	2	3	3
			5

Write the number in each box to complete the sentence

(1) 5 tens and 9 units are ☐

(2) 85 is the number you get after adding ☐ tens and

☐ units.

(3) 40 is the number you get after adding ☐ tens.

(4) The number in the tens place of 14 is ☐ and the

units place is ☐ .

(5) The number that has 2 in the tens place and 5 in the

units place is ☐ .

(6) The number that has 0 in the ones place and 3 in the

units place is ☐ .

Fill in the missing numbers to complete the sentences below

(1) The number that is 1 more than 80 is ☐ .

(2) The number that is 2 more than 25 is ☐ .

(3) The number that is 2 less than 25 is ☐ .

(4) The number that is 2 less than 80 is ☐ .

⭐ Rearrange the numbers from most to least

(1) 25 , 32 , 15 ➡ _____

(2) 81 , 18 , 28 ➡ _____

(3) 45 , 42 , 46 ➡ _____

(4) 8 , 10 , 7 ➡ _____

Fill in the missing numbers to complete the sentences below

(1) 2 hundreds, 3 tens, and 5 units are [ ]

(2) 5 hundreds and 4 tens are [ ]

(3) 7 hundreds, 9 tens, and 4 units are [ ]

(4) 9 hundreds and 7 units are [ ]

(5) 1 hundred, 1 tens, and 3 units are [ ]

(6) 2 thousands, 3 hundreds, and 6 units are [ ]

(7) 1 thousand, 5 hundreds are [ ]

(8) 3 thousands, 6 hundreds, and 5 tens are [ ]

(9) 4 thousands, 2 hundreds, and 6 units are [ ]

(10) 5 thousands and 7 units are [ ]

Dynamic subtraction (-)

Use Golden Beads or Stamp Game to learn regrouping and borrowing

		6	4
		3	9

5	2	3	4
	6	2	7

9	1	2	2
1	3	4	5

3	4	7	8
	7	8	9

	7	0	3
	2	2	4

8	7	6	3
2	9	7	5

	8	3	1
	5	7	9

		4	2
		1	9

6	2	0	4
	1	8	9

7	4	2	1
2	9	7	4

	9	0	1
	6	4	9

9	2	2	5
4	6	8	9

Dynamic subtraction (-)

Use Golden Beads or Stamp Game to learn regrouping and borrowing

	7	7	4
		9	9

6	4	1	4
	5	6	7

8	4	3	2
6	9	9	6

2	2	3	9
	8	9	9

	9	5	0
	7	6	4

5	2	4	3
1	6	5	9

	9	3	1
	7	4	8

		7	0
		3	9

4	3	1	4
	1	7	7

8	3	2	1
6	9	9	9

	7	7	0
	4	4	8

4	2	3	5
4	0	8	9

What's the Number?

Answer the number puzzle by writing the correct digit in each place value.

	Thousands	Hundreds	Tens	Units
I am a two-digit number. My units digit is 5. My tens digit is 7. What number am I?				
I am a three-digit number. My tens digit is 8. My hundreds digit is 8. My units digit is 6. What number am I?				
I am a three-digit number. My hundreds digit is 2. My units digit is 6. My tens digit is 4. What number am I?				
I am a four-digit number. My ones digit is 4. My tens digit is 8. My thousands digit is 3. My hundreds digit is 5. What number am I?				
I am a four-digit number. My hundreds digit is 6. My thousands digit is 5. My ones digit is 2. My tens digit is 8. What number am I?				

Math drills: subtraction

9 − 7	4 − 3	6 − 2	3 − 1	8 − 5
5 − 2	6 − 6	7 − 4	9 − 3	2 − 0
3 − 2	7 − 3	9 − 4	4 − 2	6 − 4
8 − 6	9 − 2	6 − 3	9 − 6	7 − 5
8 − 8	5 − 4	7 − 6	7 − 2	5 − 3

Find the missing number

Solve the equations below.

$9 + \underline{\hspace{1.5cm}} = 12$ $2 + \underline{\hspace{1.5cm}} = 8$

$5 + \underline{\hspace{1.5cm}} = 15$ $8 + \underline{\hspace{1.5cm}} = 16$

$2 + \underline{\hspace{1.5cm}} = 12$ $3 + \underline{\hspace{1.5cm}} = 9$

$7 + \underline{\hspace{1.5cm}} = 10$ $9 + \underline{\hspace{1.5cm}} = 11$

$4 + \underline{\hspace{1.5cm}} = 7$ $5 + \underline{\hspace{1.5cm}} = 13$

$2 + \underline{\hspace{1.5cm}} = 10$ $6 + \underline{\hspace{1.5cm}} = 15$

We hope this workbook has been a valuable resource for your Montessori program, whether in the classroom or at home.

⭐ ⭐ ⭐ ⭐ ⭐

Please leave us a review to help us reach a wider audience. This will enhance our product's visibility in Amazon's search results.

Check out our other products on Amazon

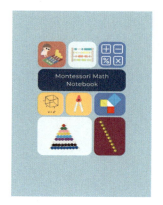

Made in the USA
Middletown, DE
29 March 2025

73462908R00067